Praise for *Adam in*

With *Adam in the Garden*, AE Hines dares to imagine a new Eden, as his speaker finds himself "middle-aged and queer," in poems that weave sound and image into tightly crafted narratives. Whether confronting betrayal and loss, sex and desire, or even environmental collapse, threads of hope and gratitude run throughout these verses, as does the speaker's anxiety about the fragility of what binds. "Perhaps you too have done this," he asks, "Found yourself awake on the edge / / of so much happiness you fear fate / might intervene?" In plain-spoken language, Hines transforms simple, everyday acts into tender and moving lyrics, offering surprising journeys and closing lines that continue to inspire. We find a poet willing to risk sentimentality without collapsing into sentiment. A seeker willing to risk blasphemy in his personal search for truth.

— Dorianne Laux, author of *Life on Earth*

AE Hines keeps giving us what we want as readers—to fall through the holes of the everyday into deeper meaning. Playful and adept in their workings, these poems are portals to hidden rooms, fields, galaxies. Even if they begin with pigeon, airplane, beloved, we find ourselves led to the Garden of All Things, the primordial place of loss and desire, taking our own bite of the apple.

— Danusha Laméris, author of *Bonfire Opera*

AE Hines is a poet of violence, wit, and the brutish assumptions of fidelity. He has a gift for describing the natural world in this latter-day garden: the pigeon's "steel / petticoat and gray patrician gown"; the tulip "boozy and voluptuous"; "a dawn congregation / of ravens" in snow. Hines understands that "hope can be given away," a truth part openness, part diminishment; *Adam in the Garden* is a subtle, skillful collection.

— Randall Mann, author of *Deal: New and Selected*

The world is fading. The Father is fading. AE Hines's *Adam in the Garden* is here to herald a new age where we "shoo / that sweet-talking serpent," accepting "nothing untrue," taking the tremulous steps of adoption, carrying a new vision for the son of men across a million unknown dangers. To build and name a new world, we each must, like Adam, recall "all the men / [we've] been" and push beyond what we have known, "edging close / to discovery." Hines will leave you longing for a paradise regained.

— J.D. Isip, author of *Kissing the Wound*

Adam in the Garden

ALSO BY AE HINES

Any Dumb Animal

Adam in the Garden

AE Hines

AE Hines

CHARLOTTE**LIT**

P R E S S

Charlotte Center for Literary Arts, Inc.
Charlotte, North Carolina
charlottelit.org

ISBN: 978-1-960558-07-7

Library of Congress Control Number: 2023952461

Cover art: "7 of Wands" by Catrin Welz-Stein (digital art)
Author photo by Brian Palacio
Book design and layout by Paul Reali

Charlotte Lit Press
Charlotte Center for Literary Arts, Inc.
PO Box 18607, Charlotte, NC 28218
charlottelit.org/press

PROUD MEMBER

[clmp]

COMMUNITY OF LITERARY MAGAZINES & PRESSES
W W W . C L M P . O R G

For Juan Diego, again

Contents

Three

Four

Angels, it seems, don't always know if they're moving among the living or the dead.

—Maria Rainer Rilke
Duino Elegies

One

Astronauts

It was dangerous then,
making love
in a Carolina backyard. First,
the hammock threatened
to flip us to the ground, taking
with it my nerve; then
you gasped at the sudden reach
of my hand, which woke
your fear, but not
our classmates asleep inside.
I spread
a blanket, and we undressed.
Silent. Back to back.
Much like we would have
in the locker room, each man
neatly piling his clothes
in opposing corners. The night
was clear, the sky knitted with stars.
We floated toward each other,
summer astronauts
on our first expedition: at first
clumsy in our experiments, each of us
taking our time as fireflies
circled our naked bodies
like blinking satellites
or distant moons, each of us
edging closer
to discovery we could not
yet name.

Breakfast in South America

A great blue-green bird follows me down
into the garden this morning, darting
from cypress to pine, sounding

four sacred notes that echo up
through the ravine like ancient calls to prayer.
It's easy—to stop and place a mango

on the low stone wall, to watch him
watching me watch him eat it. I don't know
the bird's name, neon-blue oval

crowning his head, silver-green teardrop
at the tip of his tail. But every morning
I walk out to find him waiting

among the soft ringlets of pale green moss
dripping from the trees, see beneath them
new roots raking through the dark earth

like God's own fingers. It's hard, this morning,
to see the fresh orchids, speckled yellow
and pinks bubbling up from the trunks, to see

this bird propped among the red-gold bromeliads
still fusing with the branches—to remember
this bright world, blue and green, is dying.

Small Waves

On the wet sand at sunset,
thousands of small silver fish
abandoned by the tide,
are throwing themselves
against the air toward a surf
that will not return in time.
All at once, small children
breaking free from the hands
of their parents, break
like a wave across the beach,
feet digging into tidal mud,
their small fingers scooping
and cradling each fish
before tossing it back into the sea.
The sun casts a red net
across the water's surface,
and their parents finally join in.
Perhaps out of shame. Or envy.
Perhaps they lack the heart
to explain the impossible calculus
of this task, their children holding
one quivering life
after another, each tiny death
a gift from the sea they refuse.

Adam Before Eve

Adam too walked alone in the garden,
feeding and naming the birds.

This was before Eve, before the weather
changed and leaves began to fall,

before Adam hid his dangling bits
and the down sprouting between his legs.

I wonder if he could feel the coming
change, marrow thickening

in his hastily assembled bones,
which days before had been drawn

from the river of light.
Did he notice the newborn sun

setting earlier each evening? Or
the damp smell of rot overtaking

his roses? Adam gave up on Paradise
too soon: started building parking lots

and condos. Strip malls and atom bombs.
Stopped going out each morning to shoo

that sweet-talking serpent from his yard.
Too late, once the snake's legs fell off—

four strange ornaments left hanging
in that abandoned tree.

Naturalization

We'd been lucky. I'd made it out
    of Guatemala
    alone with the baby,
and the baby still alive.

I hadn't let him crawl
    out a hotel window.
    I hadn't let him swallow
a button from my sleeve.

Managed to feed him
    and change him and carry him
    in taxis and embassies,
through markets and airports,

beneath the electric barbwire
    of US Immigration.
    In Houston, I watched
badged women and men

berate brown men in shackles
    while they sat tethered
    to stiff chairs beside us.
Most stared at their shoes.

I am embarrassed to admit
    I did nothing.
    Said nothing.
Didn't catch

a man's tired eye and offer
          even a nod, a word
          of my feeble Spanish.
Instead, I just called

my little son's name
          over and over, bouncing him
          on my lap. Then
we were ushered back

into the land I'd promised.
          Bound together by law
          and off to our next gate
without a glance back

at those men, detained,
          deported, on their way
          to whatever place
they no longer called home.

When the Muse Takes Umbrage

Not even the lesser goldfinch outside
my window so full of sun can move me,

nor the low-lying fog lounging
on the valley floor all morning, refusing

me the way I, in my youth, denied
lovers an embrace after our final release—

willing even then to share nothing
more than pursed kisses, nothing untrue.

I go in search of the honeybees banging
their cymbals, want to see them trembling

the swamp mallows in the noon sun, but find
their drums gone silent, the season already

so late. Only the narrow wasps remain.
Uninspired. Thrusting dumbly

into those last blossoms, as if oblivious
to scent. Ungrateful for color.

After the Adoption

When my lover is asleep, the wax moon
lies cradled in the black pines, swaddled light
streaming through our windows, and I creep
back to the baby. I check bedding

for loose blankets and ill-placed toys, see
that he rests flat on his back, still breathing.
Perhaps you too have done this?
Found yourself awake on the edge

of so much happiness you fear fate
might intervene. Which is to say
I am anxious when I touch my son's pink lips
with my pinkie, feel the warm air

moving in and out of his body. And why
I watch for hours as shadow and moonlight
waver from forehead to his round
dimpled cheek. By morning, I can write

a thesis on how it happens: the filling
of tiny lungs, how the fluttering wings
expand and release, rise and fall,
over and over, with no help at all from me.

Cervical Stenosis

It starts by unzipping the flesh
at the front of my neck, a six-inch
incision, the surgeon thumbing

the venous contents like a collection
of antique vinyl records. Blunt
dissection, he calls it. To push aside

trachea, esophagus,
carotid arteries. I imagine
one gloved hand wedged inside,

disappearing into the blue haze
of my throat chakra,
the metaphysical seat of expression,

mechanical pipe organ of speech.
And I can't speak: imagining him slice
the apple below my mouth, as if

parting me like soft velvet curtains
to find that small stack of bones.
I can't speak when he shows me

his silver pick, the tiny hammer, how
he will chisel away the offending disc
and pop it out like a rusty coin

stuck in the slot of a jukebox. Somewhere,
I hear music playing. Somewhere,
a woman is laughing. When he pries

apart those two dull bones, his spotlight
will shine across the bare white cord
tethering every future thing.

At the back of the stage, a small portion
of spine, naked and brave, will open
its small bone mouth and sing.

Ghost Story

Let's meet back at that thatched-roof excuse
for a hotel, perched at the edge of the sea.

Where the jungle at night lights itself
in a soft green fire, fluorescent lichens

and moss ambling across the root and trunk
of every braided tree. We wave goodbye

to the guests as the last boat leaves, and no one
can see us dancing on the terrace

disrobed of our bodies. No one knows
we're there at all, swaying

in the wind and slanted rain. At night,
the mosquitoes pass through. The bats

find no blood, and nothing can touch us
except our desire. Every night, we make love

hovering above the stiff straw bed, fold
ourselves in and out of each other. Then comes

the sun, climbing again the bamboo rafters.
And the waves go on kissing each other,

slamming the rough-shaven cliffs
that keep falling in a jumble to the sea.

To My Flirtatious Friend Who Made a Pass at My Husband on Facebook

You were right to call him beautiful.
When I first saw him, I couldn't stop
staring: those soft hazel eyes framed
by his thin wire spectacles, the fine
toothy scruff of his beard. So yes, horny devil
emoji does feel appropriate. When
I awoke after our first night, the sun up
making love to the room, I was afraid
to open my eyes, the way a drunk fears
being sober, wants to keep dreaming.
When I did, I found no evidence
he'd been there at all, the other side
of my bed so recently his, now crisp
and remade, my sleeping hand reaching
like that of the newly widowed
into empty space. Did you write *sexy*?
Oh yes. Yes indeed: one whiff
that morning of the coffee brewing
downstairs—my god—knowing
he was still here, let me tell you,
my friend, that was sexy.
I wanted him then the way the beans
long to be ground and pressed,
then pummeled by relentless steam.

The Fall

I swore I'd never go back,
                never stand at the threshold

of that carnival house
                my father called home. Never.

Where police were summoned
                and dishes went flying

and furniture ran crashing
                into walls, where people

went missing
                down the dark corridors

of their own minds.
                In its twisted mirrors

I stared at my distortion
                for years, trying to unstretch

my limbs, reattach
                my head, to find my feet

and any way out
                of its dead-end halls.

At the door, I shook
                like a near-drowned dog

to get my father out of my ears,
        to unloose my mother

(because there's always a mother)
        whose arms were locked

around my legs. When I stepped
        into the light, when my shoes

hit the road, not knowing that wherever I'd go
        for ten years, twenty,

for thirty years and thousands of miles,
        wherever I'd go

they'd be right there,
        my father's voice

repeating itself like a shrill
        and hellish clown, my mother

dragging along behind me
        like so many bags of sand—

the past, too, a carnival house—
        collapsing ceilings

and slanted floors. Wall after wall. No door.
        Not a window to be found.

Butterflies and Moths

El Retiro, Colombia

Each morning I make a bone cage
of my fingers, capture the flailing

trapped against cabinets, inside our windows,
release their flickering bodies

like confetti set loose on the wind. Of course,
most die: thrashing against the back

of my knuckles, or stuck in high places
I can't reach. Dozens litter our floors at sunrise,

fluorescent blue eyeshades, tiny emerald fans,
bright delicate winged dead and half dead

shifting in the quiet stirred breeze
of our hesitant steps. I gather these, too, each

small reflective hope swept gently into the bin,
place those still twitching on the fat branches

of orange trees beyond the reach of rain. What
do you call this foolish insistence—not

that the end not come, but that it not come
too soon? Yesterday's efforts lie

on the damp ground beneath these same branches,
silent wings the same color as the sky.

No Small Happiness

To imagine the earth will go on
without us, brings me no small

happiness. And with little faith
in God, modest comfort to believe

I might escape further judgement.
After all, what would either of us

have to say? Even as my son
hugs me goodbye this morning,

I know the ways I've failed him—
how we all keep failing, the planet's

inheritance already squandered.
They say all a man has in the end

are his memories. But I won't take
even these into oblivion. No need

for an afterlife, endless time to climb
the same regretful stairs, reliving

a life I've shoved like a grand piano
into a room too small to hold it.

Such a pleasure to know I'll be gone.
Whittled away to nothing, and yet

still crawling in whatever low creature
survives in this world to crawl:

cockroach and silverfish, the simple ant.
Why does it bring me such peace,

this notion of disappearing? To know
when Jesus spoke of the meek,

He didn't mean us.

Sacramento 1994

My neighbor wasn't wrong that Sunday she called
the cops, said she feared the young man upstairs

murdered by some other man. I did die that summer—
a hundred tiny deaths—and cremated my shame.

When I opened my door, two lady officers stood
badged in black, one waving a finger

at my half-open boxers, at my guest who came
and wrapped his arm around my waist, wearing nothing

but a towel. Was it wrong? To climb the trellis
of each man's body like a vine? I wanted to leap off and fly

the wide-open sky of my own body that summer,
to Peter Pan my way through every coffee shop

and light-dazzled bar. So when the cop said
"You boys go right on having a wonderful day,"

we did. Their black and white pulled away, and I
leaned out my second story window, two strong hands

gripping my two strong hands gripping the sunbaked sill,
opened the grateful cavity of my throat, and crowed.

Two

Written for a Friend

With the children grown, she fills
their home with snake plants and jade,
all the things that thrive on neglect.

For awhile, it's enough: stifled kisses
at their door when he leaves
each morning, therapy on Thursdays.

At night, melatonin, two drops
of valerian on the tongue. The truth
keeps its distance, clear as unfinished

dreams at sunrise, house smelling
of primrose and sage, the lingering
scent of another woman.

Sometimes, she cannot read the words
her heart keeps writing—the marriage,
not in trouble, but over. Hope,

like smoke in the eye, blurs, robs her
of context, and blinking, she averts her gaze
the way the old saints must have, when

the angel of the Lord interrupted them
mid-sentence, revealing His unstoppable
message in splendor and light. Temporary

blindness not the point, but side effect
of prophesy. Not rain, but flood.
Her husband, not going, but gone.

Green Satin

for Ginny

Perhaps, it's not the drugs
when you tell me you plan
to come back as a tree, wearing

green satin gowns and scarves
made of wind. No more ridiculous,
you say, than dying, or your wig

teetering from the nightstand.
Last night, a cypress lifted its dark
roots from the earth, and lay down

like a great, leafy-maned beast
across your yard, making room
for more morning

to flood your window, dawn
a spotlight across a hospice bed
where you labor over breathing,

a potter over clay, spinning
and kneading the mud of yourself
into finer and finer pieces.

"It must be time," you tell me,
with summer's sun shining
and the sparrows flinging

shadows on your walls.
When even the cypress lies down
and points the way home.

The Devil and the Bartender

I serve the booze, but know
never to play cards—he always wins,
and every man here owes him money.
He's good to have around—
all those sweaty jokers coming in thirsty
to cut their deals, clamoring to refill
empty pints and vacant accounts.

Like the rest of them, he can't shut up
about his girl troubles. Goes on
about that first woman who still won't
return his calls, can't forgive
that long-ago madness with the tree.
"Hell hath no fury," I finally say,
laying down another round.
"To forgive," he says, "divine," and then
we both laugh.

Of course, he's got his Daddy issues.
Hated the family business,
hated it so much, he went
into competition. Not the first kid
kicked out of the house, not the first
father to not understand.
But the way he talks
and talks, you can tell
he misses home. One time,

he brought the old man by.
Short, thinner than I imagined,
and although he smiled when I spoke,
deaf as a rock. I poured them whiskey
and listened as the son yammered
about work, the state of the world,
then talked about the good old days
back before the fall. It broke my heart
to see how much the son cared,
how he rambled on, as if
the old man, nodding, could hear.

Ocular Migraine

Sometimes, after making love, I go blind.
This is not metaphor. The world goes dark,
always in one eye. I've learned
not to panic, just to wait, looking
lopsided out the one good eye.

It happens when coming to my feet
or if I scramble too quickly up the stairs.
My heart goes pounding, and then
a kind of contraction in the head, a shade
pulled down like an eyelid I can't control.

The doctor opines about nerve cells
and blood vessels. Points to the evidence
on my MRI, tiny bright spots in my brain,
blotches tinged white, and I wonder
are these moments of exertion
or exaltation made flesh inside my skull?
Perhaps, he says, you're out of shape.
Or eat too much sugar.
Cut down the caffeine.

Sometimes, my head on your chest
and me back in my body—I think,
my mind is overtaken with more joy
than it's trained to handle. Pressure
builds in spasms behind my eyes,
and even in the dark I see I can't see.

Rain Myth

The people recalled water falling
like fresh tears onto greening
fields, how it slipped beneath

the earth's crusty surfaces
and slithered back to the rivers—
back when there *were* rivers—

to oceans, before the oceans, hot
and acrid, dwindled of the Coho
and Chinook they lifted

onto their gleaming plates
like a birthright. In the end, a fish
would need feet just to make it

up a river, until the rivers became
streams, and the streams just a trickle
that ran across the dry ground

like sweat down the back, as if
the earth were a woman, peeling off
layers, hot flashing past late middle age.

On Monogamy

We were six gay men by candlelight
discussing fidelity. Monogamy was a fad,
someone suggested, gone once there were drugs
to keep us alive, tossed with our obsession
for raising children, and marriage, which had led
to a thriving new industry for queer divorce.
Then someone poured out the last of the wine.
Someone else proposed firing up the hot tub.
A man (not my husband) touched my hand,
and another (not me) said honesty and trust
were more important than faithfulness.
I touched the muscled leg of my husband,
which stiffened a little, as if we were dancing
closer to a line we couldn't waltz back across.
Then someone said he'd never toss
a decades-old relationship over something
so frivolous as an affair. My husband
cleared his throat, and then the dishes.
I followed him into our kitchen, and at the sink
wrapped my arms around his chest. The washer
beneath our counter was empty, but he turned
on the tap, and handed me a towel so I could dry.
And as the men undressed and slipped
into our jacuzzi, we passed dishes between us
the way we still handled each other—gently,
each chipped plate as precious as the last.

What I Wish I'd Learned in Therapy

you will consider   more than twice

smashing   your own life

against the rocks   once you discover it's a boat

   you keep sailing   with the wrong bearing

no matter   how many times you adjust the sails

   happiness   blows in   or not   however it pleases

like wind   uncharted

   but it comes   it does come   though

there will be times you idle   listless   hurt

               rocked to sleep   rock yourself

when there is no one left to hold you   times

you are alive   you wish

you weren't   the same way you'll feel

in the end   about dying   until suddenly   you don't

   go ahead   clench your jaw   make fists   rage

at the sea   for all the good it will do

   you can believe   pray to angels   or demons

   some ancient norse god   or wish   upon that northern star imagine someone   somewhere   has

when you don't have   control

   who knows   maybe one of them will answer

   or maybe they won't   none of that matters

   you will make numberless wishes   numberless

as waves   or grains of sand   the hairs

     on your weathered head

The Night the Lights Went Out in Moore County, North Carolina

These must be dark times if you think
shooting up a substation and blacking out

the lights will shut down a drag show.
Have you ever been to a drag show?

Yes, there will be singing. Even in the dark.
Unflappable queens black-belting Beyoncé

and Madonna, hovering in the quivered
glow of bar top candles, silver beams

from a hundred mobile phones showering
them, bedazzled songbirds, lashes

glittering like wings and lifting them
from a thin nest of stars on the soft breeze

of applause and our waving dollar bills.
We've labored in the night long enough

to know how to fashion our own halos.
Make our own light. I doubt you've ever

dropped a copper penny to preserve
a vase of daises, or know a jigger of vodka

brings valentine roses back to their feet,
but know you'll find no wilting flowers here,

just at the edge of the stage. With its green
stiffened spine, the boozy and voluptuous

tulip takes no bows. With outstretched petals
outlasting gravity and death, it refuses to bend.

Find a Friend

It's like the sharpened stone flung
from David's sling

striking Goliath's head, my then
husband's glowing dot, this map

on my phone, him not at the office
or the hospital where he sees patients,

not the grocery store he frequents
for our family's provisions. The dot

marks the spot with his name
but an address I don't recognize

as any mutual friend, or known
place of business. Burns

the insistent red of a target's
bright eye, or the blood

pumping through the heart. I
can't help but hold my breath,

releasing the taut string
of the mind's bow, launching

my inquisitive arrow at that tiny circle,
which is not unlike the bullseye

I have imagined at the heart
of his heart, where I've loosed

my ersatz arrows for years, always
lodging them in the distant rings.

It could have been a feather, this
singular point of pixelated light

bowling me over. But it's a rock.
Sharp. To the softest part of my head.

Enjambment

A line changes meaning:
I love you

becomes *I love you*
but

becomes *I love you but*
I love myself

more.

To enjamb: to stride
across, to pass

beyond. Words
like the first leg

tossed over a high
fence. Straddling gravity

and time. No choice
but to pull the laggard

to the other side.

Family History

The way my mother tells it
I ran away. She didn't shove me
out the front door at sixteen.
Afterwards, she remembers my little sister
possessed by a poisonous anger
but has no recollection of dragging her
through the house by her hair.
The history of our family was oral,
repeated to herself
in the splotched bathroom mirror,
where everything came out backwards.
Backwards everything came out
of that mirror, where she repeated
our family history, with no recollection
of dragging my sister through the house
by her hair, of her own poisonous anger, or me
at sixteen, pleading at our front door.
She didn't shove me.
I ran away.

Paper Anniversary

It was the night of the Worm Moon,

low and full in the March sky, though

we couldn't see it, not under

the wool blanket of clouds. You

were standing at the counter cutting

vegetables when I offered you two

paper cranes—folded triangles

of Japanese silk print, speckled pixels

of red and gold—that caught the light

in the fine net of your palms. I wanted

to give you more: a dozen bouquets,

a dozen anniversaries, an endless river

of years, but I was fifty, you already fifty-two,

and the cranes made only of paper.

Security Deposit

Long ago, before breakfast
my first roommate in California
pulled his stiff prick from his boxers
and asked me to kiss it, as casually
as one might offer a guest a warm cup
of tea or a second pillow—a small request
of the twenty-one-year-old stray
he'd taken in without a security deposit.
Afterwards, he said it would be easier,
living together, old and young, having cut
that tension—the sex, he said, now
out of the way. He dressed for work,
and I stood at his window in nothing
but his boxers, watching him leave. I remember
the previous night's rain still dripping
from his eaves, the crape myrtles huddled
along his street nudging themselves
into color, as willing as I was to bloom.

Three

Bed

My husband despairs of my obsession
with darkness, wants me to write
happier poems the way he wishes
I'd make our bed when I roll out
in the morning, long after he starts his day.
I sit above a small white sea
scattering biodegradable ink across
this recycled page, but can't help thinking
of the widow next door who tells me
it's little things that piss her off now: him
not being there to make their bed together,
how each day she pulls the sheets
up around his cold pillow, then is unable
to make it through the morning paper
without him there passing her page
after page. "Bad news anyway," she says.
Wars, pandemic, sunrise
turning her windows red. Some mornings
she stares at his photo at the edge
of her breakfast table, young and handsome,
and it's enough to send her
crawling back into bed.

The Crow

I was on the phone when the crow perched
by my window this morning, flashed its wings
against the glass, then slid off
into the upper stories of a winter tree.
And the person I was speaking with
couldn't know I'd stopped listening to her,
or that I'd been drawn to my window
trying to spot the last black feathers slipping
into the leaves, splendidly green
and laden with snow, or that the crown
pointed straight to the ghost of a moon
lingering in a sky so wide it might break
open her heart if only she'd been here to see it.
We'd been speaking of forgiveness, how when
we finally get around to it, the people
we most need to forgive are gone. How others
won't return our calls. And I knew this was important
and true. That I should hang up, set about making
a list, start dialing up the past: my parents
and ex-lovers, all the neighbors I failed
to help or who failed to help me, old friends
I'd neglected, then lost. But by then
my friend was unreeling her own list
into my ear, then black talons and wings. A sky
so bright and blindingly blue, icy thumbprint
of the moon just ripe for the eye's taking.

House of the Spirits

You tell me houses here, high in the Andes,
have souls and desires of their own
and might reject a new owner the way
a body might refuse
the transplanted heart.

That first night, rains come rivering
through our slanted ceilings
and down the concrete walls.
Lights flicker then fade.

We move room to candlelit room
in rituals from your childhood:
you sprinkling dark corners with water
blessed by the village priest, me
burning incense and waving
a smoking wand of sage.

I no longer understand the mechanics
of belief. Or believe
our petitions are heard—
even here—this far up in the sky.

All night, the rain keeps falling.
Our fissured roof creaks and moans.
I lie awake listening, certain it's nothing
but the day's heat giving up,
flying off into the void.

Winter in Colombia

Just like that, another morning.
Each new day measured out
in equal hours of light, and

your most significant worry
watching the sun slice rain clouds
and sky to blue ribbons,

rainbows draping the green
rolling hips of the mountains.
Of course, bad things can happen:

your dog hit by a truck bringing
the morning eggs, fresh and stuck
with feathers. Maybe your husband

runs off with the man who delivers
mangos to your door. But mostly
the days idle along in birdsong

and fruit sauce, the hum of stingless bees.
And all you want—more mornings
outside your door, shafts

of golden light, wild spectrum cast
like a net over the wet trembling leaves
of bright-barked eucalyptus.

On the Nature of Time

I am fifty when I understand time
        as a threadbare hammock, busy

loosening, slipping itself free,
        how it threatens to unravel

and spill me across the broken ground.
        There are worse things. Finding

myself caught, again, a body
        suspended in the garden,

swimming through time's woven folds.
        I am fifty when a doctor

pulls from my inflamed anus
        twelve polyps, like twelve

angry apostles drawn
        reluctantly into the light,

tells me come back in a year,
        see which might be my

Judas. A year seems a long time
        to wait. Then no time at all,

as I go on swaying to stillness
      in the gathering shadow, sun

bleeding across the sky
      like stone rolled from a tomb.

Hummingbird

My veins quicken with my first

      dose of coffee, and I watch a small prince,

from green lamé crown to trembling tail, bow

      at our feeder in a blurred halo of wings.

Forgive me my disclosures, my naked

      thirst and need for description.

I can still feel the echo of the night,

      you, ebbing like a current through my body,

warm aftershock of me in yours; the center of me

      vibrates at the sight: royalty bowing

before a long glass cylinder, tall, brimming

      with light, such lecherous gulps swelling

his violet throat when he dips his whetted beak

      into the rising tear of its yellow eye.

Anxiety Disorder

on a plane at 30,000 feet

When the worst happens, you find

yourself strangely centered, as if some

elusive chord has been struck

and a woeful sound you've always expected

goes vibrating through your body. The voice

of our pilot floating through the air

attempts to calm us, says

the plane's hydraulics are shot,

but not to worry, we'll be landing

on foam. And I think: *Yes. Yes, of course.*

As if I've been waiting for precisely this.

As if I am greeting a disheveled friend at my door,

not thinking of those gigantic black wheels

held like undescended testicles, useless

in the round, steel belly of that plane.

I Give My Friend My Totem

Before my divorce, my body
a wilderness, my first husband off
exploring somebody else's, I carry
in my pocket a small, heart-shaped stone
stained bright as a cartoon sun, the word
HOPE chiseled in bold letters across
its two halves.
              It helps, for a while,
feeling its weight shift against my leg
when I move from the car
to the therapist's office, and when I
can't breathe, thrusting my hand
into the deep well of denim to find
its cool surface, the cut letters
beneath my fingers, imagining
one can shift the ballast
in another man's heart.
              I don't see it
until years later—the obvious metaphor.
Heart made of stone. How hearts
like stones can sink. By then, the rock
a paperweight I keep on the corner
of my desk, reminder of my resilience.
That not every heart must be broken.
And hope can be given away.

Fat City Pigeon

In a terrace garden, twenty-two stories up

against the pastel dawn, you squat on a rail

while I dangle my feet above this small bed

of green, feeding ravenous plants the thin

clippings of my toenails. I ask myself why

I have judged you as ugly. With your steel

petticoat and gray patrician gown, you

could be my great-grandmother, lounging

in her jeweled necklace of amethyst and jade.

Have you come back to sell me on Heaven?

As you lift and shake out your arthritic wings,

the sun splinters and ripples across a valley

pillared with glass. Heaven nowhere

but here. The city revving its engines.

Death, in the distance, rehearsing her song.

The First Time She Goes Missing

My sister and I call out to our mother,
lost in the Carolina pines, swimming
in her own private darkness where

green needles shimmer in the soft
purple twilight. This, how a child
learns to pray. Air too sweltering

for sleep, in this way a new protector
forged from a son. A man who will
lay back the darkness in spite of his fear.

Who has learned to wait for dawn
to pass again across her eyes. Even now,
I imagine her gone to the black recesses,

sinking into the loamy soils. Sometimes,
late in the night, I hear her crying out
at the moon as it slices through the trees.

Heliconian

This morning, a spotted orange butterfly
touches down on my shoulder, and I forget

       for a moment one side of the earth
       shimmies and burns, and on the other,

fresh floods sally away great swaths
of land. I forget the sun in places shines

       its merciless face on dry soils crying out
       for rain. I want to name it, this moment

of forgetting. Of believing there's any
coming back for us. When this tiny

       brush-footed muse lifts off, she grazes
       the short peak of my nose, waves

her brief shadow across my eyes, leaving
me here, astonished by all this light.

Postcard from the Dead

Ten years later, my killers
          interviewed from their cells
will say: M*atthew Shepard*

needed killing. Ten years after that,
          my people lay my ashes
to rest in the shining capitol,

under the stone ceiling
          of a vaulted cathedral, far
from the fence in that naked winter field,

from the icy prison of Wyoming.
          My killers thought I'd be forgotten
when they offered me a ride, then

bound my hands and placed
          that filthy bag over my head.
But for twenty years, for thirty, far longer

than I was alive, our people remember
          my name. It blooms
from their lips like a cold prairie rose.

Eden

I recall placing ripe plantain on the lowest
branch of eucalyptus, and the tree
filling with small wings: toucans
and motmots, a flock of miniature finches
dusted with pale blue chalk. There are so few
days I would—if I could—set on repeat
and live over and over.
                Here, the man
I love, sight of him a reviving breath,
carrying plates of chorizo and fried eggs.
Then the two of us reclined in dappled grass,
drinking hot chocolate from a single,
chipped cup beneath prehistoric ferns
that tower and sway just as they must have
with the world still new.
                I liked to pretend
then too—didn't I?—that we were the first
and last of our kind, a multitude
of wings beating the air under a sun
that never set, our queer, middle-aged bodies
never a day older.

Four

Adam in Another Garden

He stands above rows of spring lettuce,
        staring down as he has for weeks,
                confused that his small mounds

of iceberg and rocket refuse to grow,
        as if one of the boys were taking
                his clippers and mowing down

in the night whatever meager
        new leaves sprouted that day.
                Things would have been different

had Eve been in *this* garden,
        when Adam discovers
                the small gray-white rabbit

living in their stacked rock wall.
        The worst part of all—
                how the bunny comes right to him,

nose edging forward, twitching
        from the shadowed hole, how
                it hops to Adam's open hand

when the master gardener calls.
        It doesn't look up
                or flatten its ears, when

with his other hand, Adam pulls a single
        jagged stone from the top of the wall.
                And though Abel has run off,

screaming for his mother, Cain sees it all.
        When that rock comes down,
                Cain is standing right there.

Incarnation

Before the body, Father, I was the lust
in your myopic eye, sigh
of that coy child, the lunch counter
waitress who fetched you coffee
and fried egg sandwiches for the months
it took her to decide. Back then,
I was still dust—ash rising
in my own private universe of chlorophyll
and sun—until I was the dust
sucked up into her cornbread
and boiled okra, odds and ends
she used to weave me into me, tootsie rolls
and peanut butter cups, sun-steeped
iced tea she balanced on her ripening belly
as I quietly willed myself into flesh.
You think you made me, Father? Taking
that girl, slight and virginal, wedding her
across state lines where officials asked
no questions, then breaking her like a horse
when she begged for tenderness, pleading
for a hospital when the bleeding wouldn't stop.
They say the dead should hold their peace,
but what do they say of the not-yet-breathing,
who stand and watch from the gate? Who fall
backwards into this world from their wombs
to open their mouths and speak.

Fibrillation

I think of my friend Phillip,
                his forty-four-year-old body

dropping to the cold gym floor,
                not to give his trainer twenty,

but his heart forgetting to beat, once
                steady wings in his chest

silent for the first time.
                It isn't so much that he died,

but was reborn, after the panicked man
                clamped his pink lips to blue,

and the EMT used paddles to wake
                Phil's sleeping heart with fire.

Most days, this makes me remember
                to palm my own, fingers

spread and listening to my own
                fluttering bird, as each

breath leaves this body, and like a small
                resurrection, returns.

The Exhibitionist

Somedays I long to be touched
        in public. In my most private places.
Somedays I wake so grateful to have

this body, knees just starting to go,
        capillaries blooming like strange galaxies
across skin that daily falls

a little closer to the earth. It's not a hangover.
        No, Darling. This, just how the body
feels now. And yet, I'm grateful to have a lover,

one I'd like to grab by his hand this morning
        and walk undressing into the widest
clearing of Freedom Park, both of us sinking

to the sun-drenched ground, our fingers
        and tongues working like libidinous keys
into every soft, relenting lock. It's not

too late, is it? Asses rising in the air
        like willing loaves of bread. I long
to be broken. Want to be served. To make

grass wet with our sweat and tremble
        the ground so that they hear us, and
when they hear us, even the dead wake.

On a Bench by Little Sugar Creek

for Matt

A friend's death reaches me
on an afternoon I am staring
at scrub trees—skinny laurels,
red-berried hollies—and sitting
on a park bench raking my thoughts
like a drift of fallen leaves.
In winter's light, the actual leaves
seem dusted in gold, air cold
but still tolerable in my down jacket.
Other benches dot the creekside,
all empty, with bronze plaques
bearing names—people loved
well enough to be remembered
with steel and concrete, stiff wooden planks.
My friend is dead. Too young. Too
everything. Two baby boys, a husband
who loved him. My friend is dead
and I think I should get up
and do something. Not just sit here
on this bench, memorial to a man
I never met, by this sloped bank of rocks
that spill into clay-stained water, small birds
rummaging piles of decay.

A foot of new snow

and down the middle
        of our icy street
a dawn congregation
        of ravens, all blue-black
and wing, hunch
        in their strange bureaucracy,
as if arrived to divide
        the daily assignments. Even
at this age, I still see signs. Even
        a gathering of black birds
on a snow-covered road,
        a Rorschach test
that conjures a warning
        in my anxious machinery:

an assembly of plague doctors—
        with folded feather arms, dark
nodding heads. I wonder what
        they are here to tell me.
None of us is promised green lights
        and straightaways, but sometimes
the bloodwork comes back
        quietly, the tumor
benign. Sometimes, just up the road
        from where you lie in bed,
brakes give way and barrel
        a terrified trucker across four
frozen lanes into your
        could-have-been path.

Red-Eye Out of Atlanta

I'm waiting with our bags when you emerge

from the men's room, gliding as you do, effortless

across that rough sea of 3 a.m. faces.

Perhaps it's the jet lag. Or that I'm sleep-deprived

and still drunk on new love. But your hands, wet

from the faucet, your fingers glistening beneath

the dull hum of that airport light, glint

of the ring I placed there, and suddenly

I'm pulled forward the way a slow barge might

be drawn through a narrow canal, tugged along

behind you through that slough of sleepwalking

bodies. Feeling what, exactly? Safe? Yes. And happy

when you take my tired hand on our next flight,

and our next, holding it until I close my eyes.

Signal Fire

My gentle queries pile up
on the little blue clouds
of a towering one-sided text

with my newly adult son. I've
fallen in love with his one-word replies,
grown hooked on his ellipses, those

three blinking dots strobing left to right
which too often disappear with no message,
no new green bubble bearing his name,

no sturdy *whoosh-whoosh, tap-tap*
vibration in my hand—a weak
substitute for proximity.

This what it means, now, to be
in touch. Across the jagged mountain
of days, gray-white circles glow

like far-off fires. And every fortnight
a carrier pigeon coos and teeters
in the soft flesh of my palm.

Aubade

I'd like to make the argument love
is enough, that twelve bridges, heart
sutured by steel and wood lacing

the Columbia to the Willamette, could
always draw us back together. They say
the more we adore a thing, the more

names we give it: *Sweetie, Babycakes.*
Bridgetown. Stumptown. City
of Roses. In Jamison Square this evening,

a woman feeds a flurry of pigeons. Birds,
she tells me, her truest friends, as she hoists
a wet mash of corn over her head

like a torch thrust above a blue sea
of tents, raises it into cracks of a sky
pierced by concrete and glass, condominiums

now empty, turning their backs. A rush
of gray and purple feather blurs the air.
Two friends settle on her shoulders.

What the street woman knows: everything
with a body will compromise to eat,
must piss and shit wherever there's a place.

A chorus of cauldrons, rusted-out drums,
blaze up in the night, embers flying out
into darkness like prayers

that quickly burn out. It isn't that I
didn't love you. *PDX. Rip City.*
I loved you, *Portlandia,*

like a drowning woman swallowed
by the river, a woman loved
by a man unable to swim.

We sit upright and bound

in the sweaty sheets of afternoon,

watching black vultures rise

past the balcony, circle the soft haze.

Rain is coming, another storm I hear

call across the eastern mountains.

A soft gray billows into the sky,

faintly rumbles

like the echo of faraway cannons.

Touching your skin is stealing fire.

Electric, this thing I am chasing.

Lips to flesh. First tingle of fingertips

as our hands tear away the covers.

That first clap of thunder.

The static inside our bodies, lightning

fixing its gaze on the ground.

Winter Memory

Once, on the twenty-sixth
      of December, my mother

and father, baby sister and I
      stepped from our shoes,

rolled pants to the knees,
      and waded into the shallow

eddies of a forest creek.
      Winter was upon us,

but a southeast winter, cold
      then muggy, sunny, then

a sky shrouded and cold again,
      pressure building like truth

behind the tongue
      in a child's guilty throat.

We held hands, one family
      in those gentle swirls, water

currenting about our ankles, watched
      as a deer and her fawn drank

safely on the other side. Such a rare
      silence—for a people

who never knew peace. By morning
    that creek had frozen over,

the small ripples from our upturned toes
    carried off and lost downstream.

Blizzard

My car abandoned in a ditch, I walk in too-thin clothes
watching neighbors help neighbors shovel gravel

beneath their wheels. I hold a stranger's hand as we
slide across ice, past other strangers' cars that slide

helplessly together like slapstick comedians—blocking
the road, making laughable any call for a tow. Then, night

silent and frozen, we go blind and plodding single file
through a slanted veil down Burnside. She sinks

each foot into holes plumbed by mine. We wipe flakes
from our eyes, and small mounds rise from our shoulders.

Maybe this is what it's like to die. Passing beneath the quieted
firs caked in white. Finding no taxis or Ubers or Lyfts, no buses

waiting at bus stops. Not even a working streetlamp. Maybe
Death, the one stranger there to guide you in the silence,

offering a small wave as he departs without a word, and you
wade off in the darkness, searching for your own front door.

On Leaving

I wanted to see the magnolia tree, pink blossoms
unfurled on twisted limbs, heavy and bursting,

wanted to cradle a low hanging bloom in my hand
again—before we sold and packed up the house,

which kept watch over that city still dreaming
of spring when we left it. New voices

would be singing inside those walls when the tree
opened its eyes, new feet walking summer's carpet

of dead petals. Mostly, I think we want to stop
wanting: the past, our futures. For just

an afternoon to nap beneath the bark wings
of a magnolia, waking in the leafy gaps

to sun and a silver shard of sky. Wake,
and without looking back, walk away.

Some Quiet Evenings

I go out to sit with them—thin
insects tuning their strings,
the night's first bat casting
in the breeze—and remember
that evening, hot and windless,
a new lover stripping
my bed, spreading my sheets
on the moonless grass.
Who were we then?
Young and swallowed
by the night. Unfinished.
Ill matched.
Sirius trudged across
my narrow field of sky,
the whole universe sliding
away, a little more life
slipping out of me, again
so briefly in love.
Some quiet evenings I go out
to sit with them, all the men
I've been, and beneath
that same quilt of stars retrace
my path, the weak orbit
of every man to touch me.

Notes

The opening line of "The Night the Lights Went Out in Moore County, North Carolina" alludes to the line "In the dark times / will there also be singing?" by Bertolt Brecht. The poem is written in response to a December 2022 domestic terrorist attack on the electrical power grid in rural North Carolina, rumored to be motivated by widespread anti-LGBTQ+ protests against a local drag show performance which was underway at the time of the outage.

The title of the poem "Heliconian" alludes both to Heliconius, the colorful and widespread genus of brush-footed butterflies, and also to Mount Helicon, which ancient Greeks believed to be the home of the Muses.

The poem, "Postcard from the Dead," is an elegy for Mathew Shepard, who on October 7, 1998, was targeted and brutally attacked for being gay, then tied to a fence in a field outside of Laramie, Wyoming where he was left to die. The quote, "Matthew Shepard / needed killing," is taken from interviews with his convicted murderers, Aaron McKinney and Russell Henderson, as presented in a 2009 epilogue to the play "The Laramie Project," developed by New York's Tectonic Theatre Project.

Acknowledgments

Much gratitude to the editors of the following publications in which these poems or earlier versions, sometimes with different titles, first appeared:

Alaska Quarterly Review: "Breakfast in South America"

Crab Creek Review: "Ocular Migraine"

The Greensboro Review: "Sacramento 1994"

I-70 Review: "Adam Before Eve," "Butterflies and Moths," "The Crow," "A foot of new snow," "On Leaving," "On the Nature of Time," "Rain Myth," "Red-Eye Out of Atlanta"

Litmosphere: Journal of Charlotte Lit: "After the Adoption," "Find a Friend"

Little Patuxent Review: "House of the Spirits"

Ninth Letter: "Ghost Story"

Palette Poetry: "Security Deposit"

Poet Lore: "Enjambment," "What I Wish I'd Learned in Therapy"

Qu: "Family History," "Paper Anniversary"

Rattle: "The Night the Lights Went Out in Moore County, North Carolina"

Rhino: "Cervical Stenosis"

South Florida Poetry Journal: "On Monogamy," "Postcard from the Dead," "To My Flirtatious Friend Who Made a Pass at My Husband on Facebook"

The Southern Review: "Astronauts"

The Sun: "Some Quiet Evenings"

Tar River Poetry: "Naturalization"

Windfall: "Blizzard"

"The Devil and the Bartender" was published in the *Montreal International Poetry Prize Anthology* (McGill University Press, 2020).

"The Fall" was published in *Our Silent Voice: Break the Silence* (Our Silent Voice, 2021).

"Security Deposit" was first place winner of *Palette Poetry's* 2022 Love and Eros Prize, selected by Carl Phillips.

I wish to thank my husband, Juan Diego, for his love and support. He patiently listened and responded to every poem, encouraged me when I was lost, and kept me fed in every sense of the word.

Thanks also to my son, Ethan, for continuing to inspire.

Forever and always, to my mother in poetry, Andrea Hollander, for her close reading and consideration of the initial manuscript.

Additional gratitude to Pacific University's MFA program where many of these poems were written or workshopped, especially to Dorianne Laux, Joseph Millar, Shara McCallum, Kwame Dawes, and Mahtem Shifferaw, and, most of all, to Danusha Laméris for her generous feedback on my thesis, which later became this book.

Thanks to José A. Alcántara, Emily Ransdell, Jeanne Yu, Todd Turnidge, Brennan Staffieri, Chrys Tobey, Justin Rigamonti, James Crews, Sarah Creech, Dion O'Reilly, Morri Creech, Richie Hofmann, and JD Isip for their feedback and support.

Sincere gratitude also to Kathie Collins, Paul Reali and everyone at Charlotte Lit Press, for selecting the manuscript for publication, and for their incredible sensitivity and support while steering this book to completion.

About the Author

AE Hines is the author of *Any Dumb Animal* (Main Street Rag, 2021). He has won the *Red Wheelbarrow* Prize and *Palette Poetry*'s Love and Eros Prize, and has been a finalist for the Montreal International Poetry Prize. His poems have been published in such journals as *The Southern Review, Prairie Schooner, Rattle, The Sun,* and *Alaska Quarterly.* His literary criticism can be found in *American Poetry Review, Rain Taxi, and Northwest Review.* He received his MFA from Pacific University, and resides in Charlotte, North Carolina and Medellín, Colombia. Online: aehines.net.

Printed in the USA
CPSIA information can be obtained
at www.ICGtesting.com
CBHW032250230224
4616CB00004B/23